For You . . . With Love.

This journal is my most intimate gift to you. It is a record of my memories—memories of you and of many special people who played a part in making you the unique and wonderful person you are today.

As you read it, I hope you come to know me, our family, and even yourself more deeply than ever before.

Time has a way of diluting our memories, even those we hold most dear. Consider this journal your strongest defense. Some of the stories I've included here will be familiar to you, and others may be a surprise. I hope all of them give you pleasant memories of your family for many years to come.

This journal is presented to

_____

On the occasion of

_____

Date

_____

With love from

_____

MARY ENGELBREIT

www.maryengelbreit.com

and Mary Engelbreit are registered trademarks
of Mary Engelbreit Enterprises, Inc.

04 05 06 07 EPB 10 9 8 7 6 5 4 3 2 1

ISBN: 0-7407-4148-9

Design by Stephanie R. Farley
Edited by Polly Blair

ATTENTION: SCHOOLS AND BUSINESSES
Andrews McMeel books are available at quantity discounts with
bulk purchase for educational, business, or sales promotional use.
For information, please write to: Special Sales Department,
Andrews McMeel Publishing, 4520 Main Street, Kansas City, Missouri 64111.

A COLLECTION OF FAMILY MEMORIES

Illustrated by Mary Engelbreit

Written by Catherine Hoesterey

**Andrews McMeel
Publishing**

Kansas City

Contents

chapter one

Where You Come From

Your Great-Grandparents
Your Mother's Maternal Grandparents

My grandfather's name: _____

_____

He was born (place/date): _____

_____

My grandmother's name: _____

_____

She was born (place/date): _____

_____

They were married in: _____

_____

After marrying, they lived in: _____

_____

_____

_____

_____

My grandparents earned their living: _____

_____

_____

_____

My strongest memories of my maternal grandparents are: _____

_____

_____

_____

_____

_____

An interesting thing about their lives was: _____

_____

_____

_____

_____

_____

_____

Your Great-Grandparents
Your Mother's Paternal Grandparents

My grandfather's name: _____

_____

He was born (place/date): _____

_____

My grandmother's name: _____

_____

She was born (place/date): _____

_____

They were married in: _____

_____

After marrying, they lived in: _____

_____

_____

_____

_____

My grandparents earned their living: _____

_____

_____

_____

My strongest memories of my maternal grandparents are: _____

_____

_____

_____

_____

_____

An interesting thing about their lives was: _____

_____

_____

_____

_____

_____

_____

Your Great-Grandparents
Your Father's Maternal Grandparents

Dad's grandfather's name: _____

_____

He was born (place/date): _____

_____

His grandmother's name: _____

_____

She was born (place/date): _____

_____

They were married in: _____

_____

After marrying, they lived in: _____

_____

_____

_____

_____

His grandparents earned their living: _____

_____

_____

_____

The strongest memories he has of his maternal grandparents are: _____

_____

_____

_____

An interesting thing about their lives was: _____

_____

_____

_____

_____

Your Great-Grandparents
Your Father's Paternal Grandparents

Dad's grandfather's name: _____

_____

He was born (place/date): _____

_____

His grandmother's name: _____

_____

She was born (place/date): _____

_____

They were married in: _____

_____

After marrying, they lived in: _____

_____

_____

_____

_____

His grandparents earned their living: _____

_____

_____

_____

The strongest memories he has of his maternal grandparents are:

_____

_____

_____

_____

An interesting thing about their lives was: _____

_____

_____

_____

_____

_____

Your Grandparents
Your Maternal Grandparents

My father's name: _____

_____

His brothers and sisters were: _____

_____

_____

He was born (place/date): _____

_____

As a young man, he liked to: _____

_____

_____

His education: _____

_____

_____

He earned his living by: _____

_____

_____

His interests and accomplishments included: _____

_____

_____

_____

_____

Some of the stories he told me about his childhood: _____

_____

_____

_____

_____

_____

_____

_____

Men are what
their mothers made them.
—Ralph Waldo Emerson

My mother's name: _____

_____

Her brothers and sisters were: _____

_____

_____

She was born (place/date): _____

_____

As a young woman, she liked to: _____

_____

_____

Her education: _____

_____

_____

She worked as a: _____

_____

_____

_____

Her interests and accomplishments included: _____

_____

_____

Some of the stories she told me about her childhood: _____

_____

_____

_____

_____

_____

_____

_____

My parents met: _____

_____

_____

They were married: _____

_____

_____

For their honeymoon, they: _____

_____

_____

Their first home was: _____

_____

_____

As a young couple they spent a lot of their time: _____

_____

_____

Some of my favorite stories about their early years together: _____

_____

_____

_____

_____

_____

_____

_____

_____

_____

_____

_____

Who takes the child
by the hand
takes the mother
by the heart.
—Danish proverb

Your Grandparents
Your Paternal Grandparents

Dad's father's name: _____

_____

His brothers and sisters were: _____

_____

_____

He was born (place/date): _____

_____

As a young man, he liked to: _____

_____

_____

His education: _____

_____

_____

He earned his living by: _____

_____

_____

His interests and accomplishments included: _____

_____

_____

_____

_____

Some of the stories he told Dad about his childhood: _____

_____

_____

_____

_____

_____

_____

_____

_____

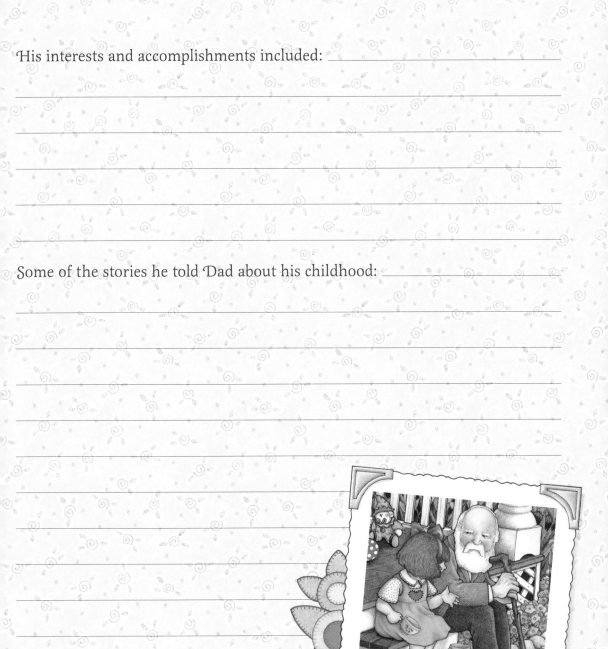

Dad's mother's name: _____

_____

Her brothers and sisters were: _____

_____

_____

She was born (place/date): _____

_____

As a young woman, she liked to: _____

_____

_____

Her education: _____

_____

_____

She worked as a: _____

_____

_____

_____

Her interests and accomplishments included: _____

_____

_____

_____

_____

Some of the stories she told Dad about her childhood: _____

_____

_____

_____

_____

_____

_____

_____

Dad's parents met: _____

_____

_____

_____

They were married: _____

_____

_____

For their honeymoon, they: _____

_____

_____

Their first home was: _____

_____

_____

_____

As a young couple they spent a lot of their time: _____

_____

_____

_____

28

Some of my Dad's favorite stories about their early years together: _____

_____

_____

_____

_____

_____

_____

_____

_____

_____

_____

_____

_____

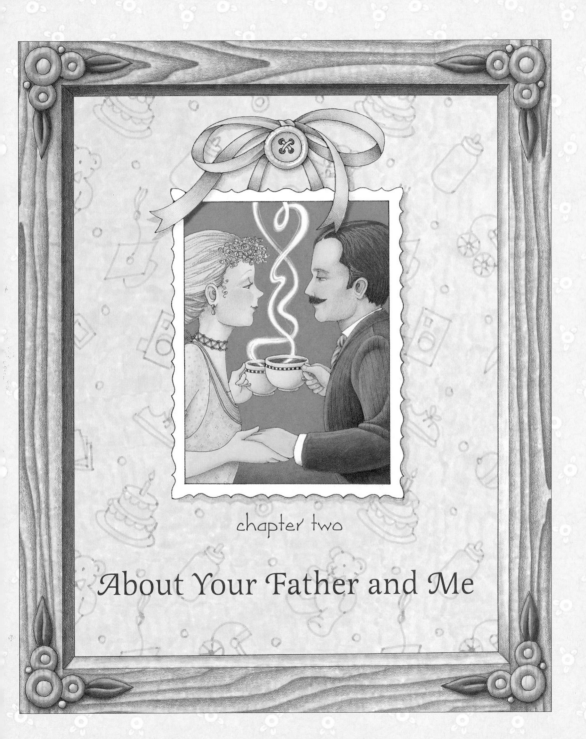

chapter two

About Your Father and Me

A Little Bit About Me

I was born (date/place): _____

I was named: _____ because: _____

_____

Other members of my family (in birth order) are: _____

_____

_____

As a young child my parents said I was: _____

_____

_____

Some of my earliest childhood memories are: _____

_____

_____

_____

When I was a child, I thought my parents: _____

_____

_____

_____

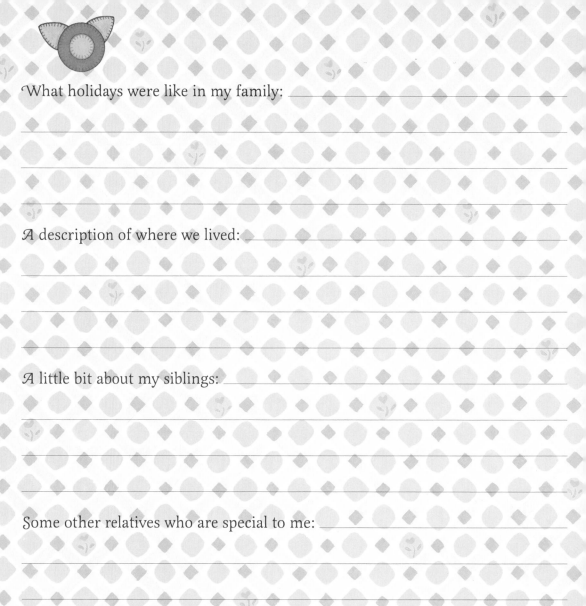

What holidays were like in my family: _____

_____

_____

_____

A description of where we lived: _____

_____

_____

_____

A little bit about my siblings: _____

_____

_____

_____

Some other relatives who are special to me: _____

_____

_____

Games we liked to play as children: _____

_____

_____

The clothes we wore: _____

_____

_____

As kids, we used to argue about: _____

_____

_____

I spent a lot of time: _____

_____

_____

Some of my closest childhood friends were: _____

_____

_____

_____

_____

_____

What it was like growing up when I was a child: _____

_____

_____

_____

When I was a child, I dreamed of: _____

_____

_____

The first person I had a "crush" on: _____

_____

As a child I remember being proud of: _____

_____

_____

My parents and I could never seem to agree on: _____

_____

_____

I once got into a lot of trouble when I: _____

_____

_____

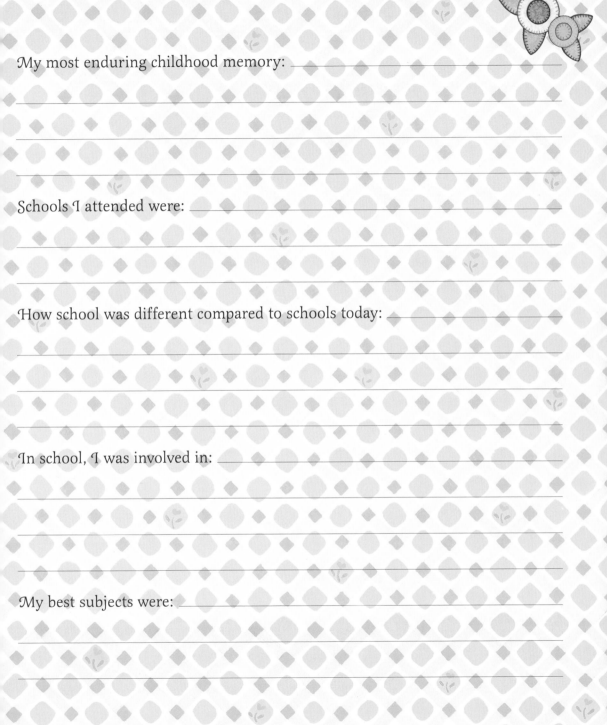

My most enduring childhood memory: _____

_____

_____

_____

Schools I attended were: _____

_____

_____

How school was different compared to schools today: _____

_____

_____

_____

In school, I was involved in: _____

_____

_____

_____

My best subjects were: _____

_____

_____

I started dating: _____

_____

On dates, we usually: _____

_____

_____

Ways I earned spending money when I was growing up: _____

_____

What radio, movies, and television were like then: _____

_____

_____

Some national and world events that had an impact on my family and how

they affected us: _____

_____

_____

_____

Growing up, I worried about: _____

_____

_____

Other comments about my childhood: _____

_____

_____

_____

_____

_____

_____

_____

_____

_____

_____

You can never really live anyone else's life,
not even your child's. The influence
you exert is through your own life,
and what you've become yourself.
—Eleanor Roosevelt

A TRUE FRIEND
IS THE
GREATEST OF
ALL BLESSINGS

Growing Up

After high school, I: _____

_____

_____

_____

About college: _____

_____

_____

_____

My first job was: _____

_____

_____

_____

_____

Something I was proud of during my early adult years was: _____

_____

_____

_____

If I could live part of my life over again, I would: _____

_____

_____

_____

The best advice my parents ever gave me was: _____

_____

_____

_____

Some not-so-good advice they gave me was: _____

_____

_____

_____

Your Father's Background

He was born (date/place): _____

He was named: _____ because: _____

_____

Other members of his family (in birth order) are: _____

_____

_____

A little bit about his siblings: _____

_____

_____

_____

Other relatives who are special to him: _____

_____

_____

_____

Some of his closest childhood friends were: _____

_____

Dad says his most enduring childhood memory is: _____

_____

_____

_____

Something you might not know about your father's childhood: _____

_____

_____

_____

When your father was a child, he dreamed of: _____

_____

_____

_____

Your father says his proudest moment as a child was: _____

_____

_____

As a child, he once got into big trouble for: _____

_____

_____

Other comments about his childhood: _____
_____
_____

Schools he attended were: _____
_____
_____

In school, he was involved in: _____
_____
_____

His best subjects were: _____
_____
_____

After high school, he: _____
_____
_____

About college: _____
_____
_____

His first job was: _____

_____

_____

_____

Something he was very proud of during his early adult years was: _____

_____

_____

_____

_____

_____

_____

_____

_____

When I First Met Your Father

Your father and I first met: _____

_____

_____

My first impression of him was: _____

_____

_____

He says his first impression of me was: _____

_____

_____

What really made him interesting to me was: _____

_____

_____

Dad says he was first attracted by my: _____

_____

I think we were a good couple because: _____

_____

We dated for: _____

_____

_____

_____

Things we liked to do together: _____

_____

_____

_____

_____

_____

_____

_____

Youth fades; love droops;
the leaves of friendship fall.
A mother's secret love
outlives them all.
—Oliver Wendell Holmes

I first thought we might get married when: _____

_____

_____

A description of the moment we decided to get married: _____

_____

_____

_____

At the time, I was thinking: _____

_____

_____

_____

The date of our engagement was: _____

_____

_____

_____

_____

In planning the wedding, some of our longest discussions were about: _____

_____

_____

_____

_____

My parents' reaction to our engagement: _____

_____

_____

_____

Your father's parents thought: _____

_____

_____

_____

Our friends thought: _____

_____

_____

_____

Our Wedding

My full name: _____

Your father's whole name: _____

Your father and I were married on: _____

At: _____

The ceremony was performed by: _____

The bridal party included: _____

_____

_____

Before the wedding, I felt: _____

_____

_____

Dad says he felt: _____

_____

_____

The wedding reception: _____

_____

My strongest memories of our wedding day: _____

_____

_____

_____

For our honeymoon we: _____

_____

_____

_____

Some additional comments about the wedding: _____

_____

_____

_____

_____

_____

_____

_____

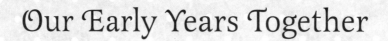

Our Early Years Together

After we were married, we lived: _____

_____

_____

_____

We spent a lot of our time: _____

_____

_____

_____

In those early years, we dreamed about: _____

_____

_____

_____

_____

Some of our close friends at that time were: _____

_____

_____

_____

During that time, Dad worked at: _____

_____

_____

_____

I worked: _____

_____

_____

_____

We sometimes worried about: _____

_____

_____

_____

About our first home: _____

_____

_____

_____

_____

_____

chapter three

Let's Talk About You!

Let's Talk About You!

When I learned I was pregnant with you, my first reaction was: _____

_____

_____

Your father's reaction was: _____

_____

_____

Memorable events during pregnancy: _____

_____

_____

Names we considered for a boy: _____

_____

Names we considered for a girl: _____

_____

To prepare for you, we: _____

_____

My due date was: _____

The Day You Arrived!

Date: _____

_____

Time: _____

_____

Weight: _____

_____

Length: _____

_____

Hair: _____

_____

Eyes: _____

_____

_____

To a mother, children are like ideas;
none are as wonderful as her own.
—Chinese proverb

your first photo

The doctor who delivered you: _____

_____

The hospital where you were born: _____

_____

We named you: _____

_____

We chose this name because: _____

_____

When I first saw you: _____

_____

_____

Dad's reaction: _____

_____

_____

People said you resembled: _____

_____

Those first few days with you: _____

_____

first year photo

Your First Year

In general, as an infant you were: _____

_____

_____

_____

Your eating and sleeping habits: _____

_____

_____

One thing that would usually make you stop crying: _____

_____

_____

A song I used to sing to you: _____

_____

You made us laugh by: _____

_____

_____

When you started eating solid food, your favorite was: _____

_____

_____

But you didn't like: _____

_____

_____

Your favorite toy was: _____

_____

_____

How other family members acted toward you: _____

_____

_____

We celebrated your first birthday by: _____

_____

_____

_____

From Baby to Preschool Child

As a baby, you were cared for primarily by: _____

_____

_____

Your first word was: _____

You seemed fascinated by: _____

_____

_____

An object that you became very attached to: _____

_____

When you were around other children, you: _____

_____

_____

_____

Once you could move around on your own, you loved to: _____

_____

_____

One time we really worried about you as a baby: _____

_____

_____

_____

At bedtime, you: _____

_____

_____

_____

_____

_____

_____

_____

_____

_____

Some memorable events in your first three or four years were: _____

_____

_____

_____

_____

Some of your strong personality traits that we noticed early: _____

_____

_____

_____

_____

_____

_____

_____

preschool photo

chapter four

Off to School

first day of school photo

Off to School

Your first school was: _____

_____

Your first teacher was: _____

_____

How you handled the idea of going to school: _____

_____

_____

_____

_____

_____

_____

_____

_____

_____

_____

On your very first day of school: _____

_____

_____

_____

After I left you on that first day, I felt: _____

_____

_____

After your first day, you told me: _____

_____

_____

_____

Your teacher told me: _____

_____

_____

At that age, you said that when you grew up, you wanted to be: ____

_____

_____

Additional notes: _____

_____

_____

_____

_____

_____

_____

_____

_____

_____

_____

Education should consist of a series of
enchantments, each raising the individual
to a higher level of awareness, understanding,
and a kinship with all living things.
—anonymous

elementary school photo

Elementary School Years

The name of your elementary school was: _____

_____

Your favorite activities during this time included: _____

_____

_____

Some of my favorite memories of you from this period were: _____

_____

_____

_____

We were especially proud of you when: _____

_____

_____

_____

Some additional comments about this time of your life: _____

_____

_____

middle school/junior high school photo

The Middle Years
Middle School/Junior High School

Your attitudes about school: _____

_____

In your free time, you loved to: _____

_____

During the summers, you: _____

_____

As you grew older, your personality really developed. My favorite things

about you were: _____

_____

_____

Clothes you wore during this time: _____

_____

_____

I first started thinking of you as a grown-up when you: _____

_____

_____

_____

I was especially proud of you when: _____

_____

_____

_____

One time when you got into big trouble was: _____

_____

_____

_____

_____

_____

Additional notes: _____

What we learn to do, we learn by doing.

—Aristotle

high school photo

High School Years

When you started high school, I remember that you were: _____

_____

_____

In high school you seemed especially interested in: _____

_____

_____

I was always impressed by your: _____

_____

_____

_____

Some special memories I have from this time in your life are: _____

_____

_____

_____

When you first started dating, I felt: _____

_____

Something you did that you didn't think I knew about: _____

_____

_____

You got into trouble once for: _____

_____

_____

You liked to talk about becoming a(n): _____

_____

_____

You were sometimes worried about: _____

_____

_____

After high school, you planned: _____

_____

_____

On your graduation day, I felt: _____

_____

_____

Additional notes: _____

_____

_____

_____

_____

_____

_____

_____

_____

_____

_____

_____

_____

A human being
is not attaining his full heights
until he is educated.
—Horace Mann

See How You've Grown!

As you've grown throughout the years, photographs of you bring back special memories. Here are some of my favorite photos along with my memories of the times they were taken.

chapter five

Family Memories

Family Memories

As a child, one thing you loved to do more than anything else: _____

_____

_____

I hope if you have kids they'll be just like you in the way they: _____

_____

_____

A gift we gave you that you seemed to like more than any others: _____

_____

_____

Some of your best Halloween costumes were: _____

_____

_____

For Mother's Day, you once gave me: _____

_____

_____

_____

One Father's Day you gave your dad: _____

_____

_____

_____

We still laugh about the time: _____

_____

_____

_____

At family gatherings you were always the one who: _____

_____

_____

_____

Additional memories: _____

_____

_____

_____

_____

_____

_____

_____

_____

_____

_____

_____

_____

Additional memories: _____

vacation photo

Vacations

Your first trip was to: _____

_____

_____

_____

As a traveler, you were: _____

_____

_____

To keep you entertained in the car, we: _____

_____

_____

Your first airplane flight was: _____

_____

_____

One of our best trips was:

Some misadventures we had while vacationing were:

Some other vacation memories I have are:

The heart of a mother is a deep abyss
at the bottom of which
you will always discover forgiveness.
—Honoré de Balzac

chapter six

Thoughts I'd Like to Share

The guiding principles in my life are: _____
_____
_____
_____
_____
_____

In dealing with others, I've learned: _____
_____
_____
_____

When I'm feeling down, I like to think about: _____
_____
_____
_____

Something that is very important to me that you may not realize: _____

_____

_____

_____

When I look at you today and think back on your life: _____

_____

_____

_____

_____

_____

What I've learned from you: _____

_____

_____

_____

_____

My greatest hope for you is: _____

_____

_____

_____

_____

_____

_____

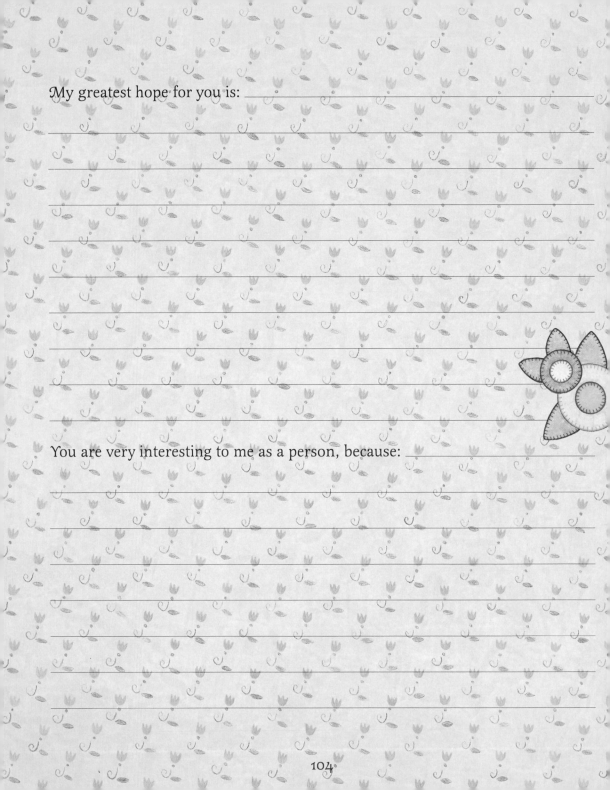

You are very interesting to me as a person, because: _____

_____

_____

_____

_____

_____

_____

_____

Other thoughts I'd like you to know: _____

_____

_____

_____

_____

_____

_____

_____

_____

_____

_____

Let's Start a New Tradition

Sharing these stories and thinking about family members and close friends who have surrounded your life has been rewarding, fun, and sometimes a little sad. I hope that you will cherish and safeguard these memories as I have.

If you've enjoyed reading this journal, you might want to keep a journal of your own memories—of all life's triumphs and struggles and day-to-day miracles. Pass it on to your own children someday. I guarantee that you'll be glad you did.

With all the love in my heart,

Keepsakes and Remembrances

Use these pages as place for souvenirs, photos, etc.

Assorted Thoughts

The End